PHYSICAL Science
AGS

Key Features:
- Includes a wealth of lab types to correspond to each Investigation Activity found in the Student Edition
- Additional follow-up questions for each lab allow you to further explore the main concept of the lab investigation
- Offers different levels of inquiry and skill practice
- Provides information on advance preparation and safety in the science laboratory

PEARSON

ALWAYS LEARNING

by
Robert H. Marshall
Donald H. Jacobs

Glenview, Illinois • Boston, Massachusetts • Chandler, Arizona • Upper Saddle River, New Jersey

ISBN-13: 978-0-7854-7070-0
ISBN-10:   0-7854-7070-0

ALWAYS LEARNING

PEARSON

PEARSON

ISBN-13: 978-0-78547070-0

ISBN-10: 0-785-47070-0

4 18

Table of Contents

Chapter 4 Classifying Elements

Chapter 5 Compounds

Chapter 6 How Matter Changes

Chapter 7 Motion

Chapter 8 Work and Machines

Chapter 9 Heat

Chapter 10 Sound and Light

Chapter 11 Electricity

Chapter 12 Magnets and Electromagnetism

Safety in the Science Laboratory

General Rules

1. Keep area clean and free of unneeded objects.
2. Do not play in the laboratory.
3. Keep equipment in good working order.
4. Wipe up spills immediately.

Heat

1. Be aware of all open flames. Flames are difficult to see on Bunsen burners.
2. Never touch flames.
3. Never touch the surface of the hotplate.
4. When heating chemicals, point test tubes away from people.

Electricity

1. Never use household current without proper supervision.
2. Remember that electricity flowing in wires causes the wires to become hot. Do not burn yourself.

Chemicals

1. Never smell chemicals directly.
2. Never taste unknown chemicals.
3. Remember that even the simplest of chemicals can cause hazardous reactions.
4. Always do chemical tests under adult supervision.
5. Do not place your fingers in your mouth while working with chemicals.
6. Always wash your hands after working with chemicals.

Safety in the Science Laboratory

General Rules

1. Keep area clean and free of unneeded objects.

2. Do not play in the laboratory.

3. Keep equipment in good working order.

4. Wipe up spills immediately.

Heat

1. Be aware of all open flames. Flames are difficult to see on Bunsen burners.

2. Never touch flames.

3. Never touch the surface of the hotplate.

4. When heating chemicals, point test tubes away from people.

Electricity

1. Never use household current without proper supervision.

2. Remember that electricity flowing in wires causes the wires to become hot. Do not burn yourself.

Chemicals

1. Never smell chemicals directly.

2. Never taste unknown chemicals.

3. Remember that even the simplest of chemicals can cause hazardous reactions.

4. Always do chemical tests under adult supervision.

5. Do not place your fingers in your mouth while working with chemicals.

6. Always wash your hands after working with chemicals.

Some Common Science Equipment

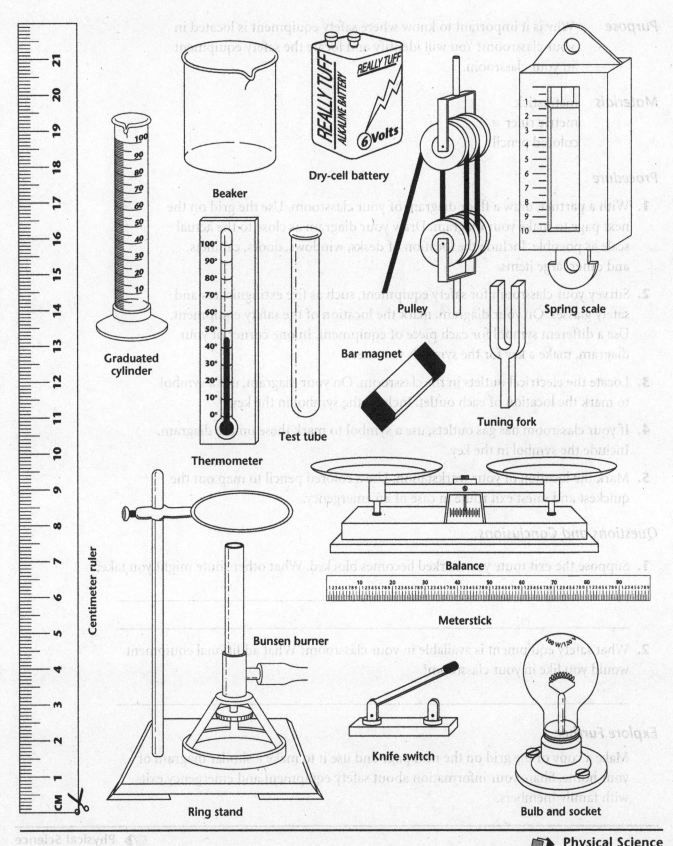

Centimeter ruler

Graduated cylinder

Beaker

Dry-cell battery

Pulley

Spring scale

Thermometer

Test tube

Bar magnet

Tuning fork

Balance

Meterstick

Bunsen burner

Knife switch

Ring stand

Bulb and socket

Safety in the Classroom

Purpose   Why is it important to know where safety equipment is located in your classroom? You will identify and locate the safety equipment in your classroom.

Materials   meterstick
metric ruler
colored pencil

Procedure

1. With a partner, draw a floor diagram of your classroom. Use the grid on the next page to make your diagram. Draw your diagram as close to the actual scale as possible. Include the location of desks, windows, doors, cabinets, and other large items.

2. Survey your classroom for safety equipment, such as fire extinguishers and safety glasses. On your diagram, mark the location of the safety equipment. Use a different symbol for each piece of equipment. In one corner of your diagram, make a key for the symbols you use.

3. Locate the electrical outlets in the classroom. On your diagram, use a symbol to mark the location of each outlet. Include the symbol in the key.

4. If your classroom has gas outlets, use a symbol to mark these on the diagram. Include the symbol in the key.

5. Mark the location of your workstation. Use a colored pencil to map out the quickest and safest exit route in case of an emergency.

Questions and Conclusions

1. Suppose the exit route you marked becomes blocked. What other route might you take?

_____

_____

2. What safety equipment is available in your classroom? What additional equipment would you like in your classroom?

_____

Explore Further

Make a copy of the grid on the next page and use it to make a similar diagram of your home. Share your information about safety equipment and emergency exits with family members.

Safety in the Classroom, continued

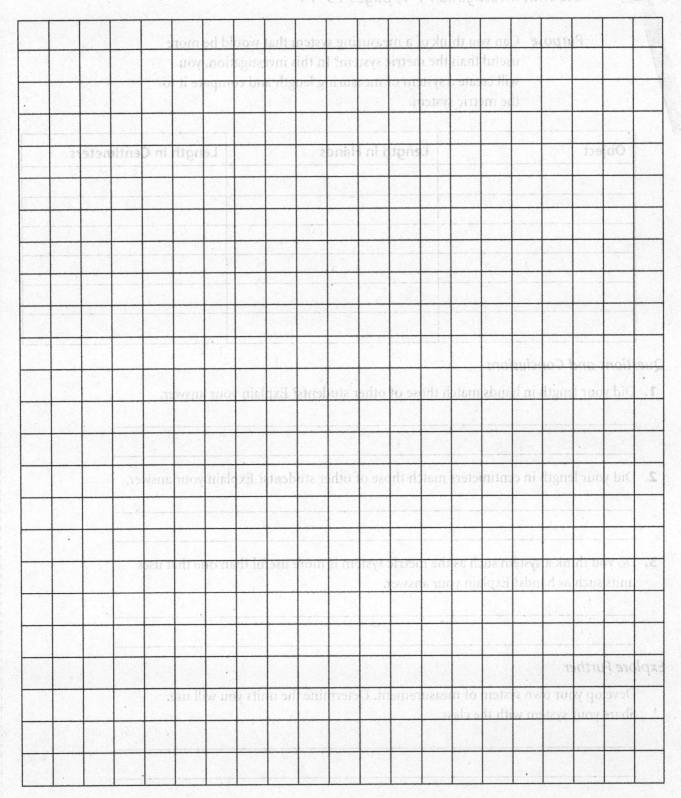

1-1 Hands Instead of Feet

Use with Investigation 1-1, pages 13–14

Purpose Can you think of a measuring system that would be more useful than the metric system? In this investigation, you will create a system of measuring length and compare it to the metric system.

Object	Length in Hands	Length in Centimeters

Questions and Conclusions

1. Did your length in hands match those of other students? Explain your answer.

_____

_____

2. Did your length in centimeters match those of other students? Explain your answer.

_____

_____

3. Do you think a system such as the metric system is more useful than one that uses units such as hands? Explain your answer.

_____

_____

Explore Further

Develop your own system of measurement. Determine the units you will use. Share your system with the class.

_____

_____

1-2 Counting Squares and Calculating Area

Use with Investigation 1-2, pages 18–19

Purpose How is area related to square units? This investigation will show the relationship between area and the number of square units.

	Length	Width	Area (length × width)	Total Number of Squares
original paper				
rectangle 1				
rectangle 2				

Questions and Conclusions

1. Does the area for the original paper in step 5 match the area calculated in step 3? Do you think it should? Explain your answer.

_____

_____

_____

2. How does the sum of the areas of the two new rectangles compare to the total number of squares in the two rectangles? How does it compare to the calculated area of the original sheet of paper? Explain these results.

_____

_____

_____

Explore Further

Repeat steps 1 through 5. Divide the grid in half. Use a ruler to draw a line from one corner to the opposite corner. Cut along the diagonal line. Measure the area of each triangle using the following formula.

$$area = base \times \frac{height}{2}$$

Calculate the sum of the two triangles. How does it compare to the area of the rectangle?

_____

_____

Finding Volume

Purpose What formula would you use to calculate volume?
You will measure objects and calculate their volume.

Materials metric ruler
rectangular boxes, such as cereal box, CD box,
toothpaste box, pizza box, shoe box, film box

Procedure

1. Use the table to record your data.

Kind of Box	Length	Width	Area	Volume (l x w x h)

2. Observe the boxes. Which one do you think has the largest volume?

_____

3. Choose one of the boxes. Write a description of the box in the first row of the data table.

4. Measure the length, width, and height of the box. Measure in millimeters
or centimeters. Record the measurements in the first row of the data table.

5. Multiply the length by the width. Then multiply that answer by the height.
The result is the volume of the box. The volume will be in cubic millimeters or
cubic centimeters. Write the volume in the data table in the last column of the first row.

6. Repeat steps 3 through 5 with the other boxes.

Finding Volume, continued

Questions and Conclusions

1. Which box has the greatest length?

   _____

2. Which box has the greatest width?

   _____

3. Which box has the greatest height?

   _____

4. Which box has the largest volume?

   _____

5. Did you correctly predict which box has the largest volume?

   _____

6. Which box has the smallest volume?

   _____

7. Do you think it is easy to predict the volume of an object just by looking at it?
   Explain your answer.

   _____

   _____

   _____

Explore Further

Arrange your boxes according to height, from tallest to shortest.
Then arrange them according to volume, from greatest to smallest.
Which boxes are in new positions?

_____

_____

_____

2-1 Identifying Properties

Use with Investigation 2-1, pages 35–36

Purpose Why is it important to provide a clear description of an object? In this investigation, you will learn to write clear descriptions of objects.

Object Number	Properties
1	
2	
3	
4	
5	

Questions and Conclusions

1. How many objects did your classmate identify correctly?

_____

_____

2. Which objects did your classmate identify?

_____

_____

3. Which objects did your classmate identify incorrectly?

_____

_____

4. What could you have done to make your descriptions more useful?

_____

_____

Explore Further

Work with five other students. Combine the objects from the bags of everyone in your group. Place objects with similar properties in a group. Identify the properties that describe all the objects in each group. Then list the property of each object in a group that makes it different from all the other objects. Elect someone in your group to share the list with the class.

_____

_____

Measuring Mass

Purpose   What equipment would you use to measure an object's mass? Use the information below to measure the mass of various objects.

Materials   balance
standard masses
penny
nickel
dime
quarter
pen
pencil
2 other small objects

Procedure

1. Use the table to record your data.

Object	Estimated Mass (g)	Measured Mass (g)
penny		
nickel		
dime		
quarter		
pen		
pencil		

2. Estimate the mass of the penny. Record your estimate in the table.

3. Place the penny in one of the pans on the balance.

4. Place standard masses in the other pan until the two sides balance. Add the masses of the standard masses to find the mass of the penny. Record this mass in the first row of the data table.

5. Repeat steps 2–4, using the other objects. Then repeat the procedure, using two objects of your choice.

Measuring Mass, continued

Questions and Conclusions

1. Which object has the most mass?

_____

2. Which object has the least mass?

_____

3. Which has more mass, the penny or the nickel?

_____

4. Which would have more mass, two pennies or the nickel?

5. How did the actual measured masses compare to your estimated masses?

_____

_____

Explore Further

Scientists use newtons to describe weight. One kilogram is equal to 9.8 newtons.
Use what you know about kilograms to convert 1,500 kilograms to newtons.
Then choose one of the objects whose mass you measured and identify its weight
in newtons. Remember, 1 gram = $\frac{1}{100}$ kilogram.

_____

_____

_____

Measuring Volume

Purpose What equipment would you use to measure the volume of an object? Use the information below to find the volume of various objects.

Materials cap from tube of toothpaste
graduated cylinder
paper towels
cap from mouthwash bottle
penny
marble
stone
game die
metric ruler

Procedure

1. Use the table to record your data.

Object	Estimated Volume (mL)	Measured Volume (mL)
toothpaste cap		
mouthwash cap		
penny		
marble		
stone		
game die—using displacement of water		
game die—using a formula		

2. Estimate the volume in milliliters of each object in the table. Record your estimates in the table.

3. Fill the toothpaste cap with water. Then pour the water into a dry graduated cylinder.

4. Read the volume of the water from the scale on the graduated cylinder. (If you need help reading a scale, use page 44 of your text.) Record the volume of the water in the table. Use a paper towel to dry the cylinder.

5. Repeat steps 3 and 4, using the mouthwash cap.

Measuring Volume, continued

6. Measure the volume of the penny, marble, stone, and game die. Use the displacement of water method described on page 47 of your text. Record these volumes in the table.

7. Use the metric ruler to measure the length, width, and height of the game die. Find the volume of the die. To find the volume, use the formula: length x width x height. Record the volume of the die in the table.

Questions and Conclusions

1. Which object has the largest volume?

   _____

2. List the objects in order from smallest volume to largest volume.

   _____

   _____

3. You measured the volume of the game die, using two different methods. Do the two volumes match?

   _____

4. How do the estimates you made in step 2 compare to the objects' actual volumes?

   _____

   _____

Explore Further

Suppose you wanted to find the volume of a cup that had a volume greater than the graduated cylinder. How could you measure the cup's volume without using additional materials? Test your procedure with a large paper cup, water, and a graduated cylinder.

_____

_____

_____

_____

2-2 Finding Density

Use with Investigation 2-2, pages 53–54

Purpose Do you think cooking oil and water have the same density? In this investigation, you will calculate and compare the densities of cooking oil and water.

Measurements	Cylinder with Water	Cylinder with Cooking Oil
A mass of empty cylinder		
B mass of cylinder and liquid		
C mass of liquid (B–A)		
D volume of liquid		
E density (E = $\frac{C}{D}$)		

Questions and Conclusions

1. Which substance—the water or the cooking oil—has the greater density?

_____

_____

2. Liquids with lesser densities will float on liquids with greater densities. If you pour cooking oil and water together, which liquid will float on top?

_____

_____

Explore Further

Corn syrup has a density of 1.3 g/cm³. If you pour corn syrup into a cylinder of cooking oil and water, what will happen?

_____

_____

Inferring the Properties of an Object

Purpose   What are the properties of a hidden object? This investigation will show that the properties of objects can be inferred from information gathered through observation of an unseen object.

Materials   clay
small object, such as a short piece of chalk, pencil eraser, or coin
paper clip
safety goggles

Procedure

1.   Use the table to record your observations.

	What I Think the Object Is Like	What the Object Actually Is Like
size		
shape		
hardness		
position		
other		

2.   🖐 Put on your safety goggles.

3.   Make a clay "atom." Form the clay into a large ball. Cut the ball in half. Place a small object between the halves, and smooth them together. Your object should now be hidden inside the clay ball.

4.   Exchange clay "atoms" with a partner.

5.   Unbend the paper clip until it is fairly straight. **Safety Alert: Handle the bent paper clip carefully.**

Inferring the Properties of an Object, continued

6. Carefully insert the paper clip into your partner's clay ball to help you get information about the object that is hidden in the ball. Some properties of the object that you should try to find out are size, hardness, and position in the clay.

7. Repeat step 6 as many times as you need to. Fill in the first column of the data table as you gather information.

8. When you have gathered as much information as possible, make a drawing on another sheet of paper showing what you think the clay "atom" looks like inside.

9. Carefully open the clay ball to reveal the object. Fill in the second column of the table.

Questions and Conclusions

1. Were you able to infer the correct size of the object?

_____

2. Were you able to infer the correct shape of the object?

_____

3. Were you able to infer the correct hardness of the object?

_____

4. Were you able to infer the correct position of the object?

_____

5. Which property was the easiest to infer?

_____

6. Which property was the hardest to infer?

_____

Explore Further

Discuss with your partner the process you used. How is identifying properties more difficult when you cannot see the object? How is this investigation like the work of scientists who have identified properties of atoms?

_____

_____

_____

3-1 Breaking Down Water

Use with Investigation 3-1, pages 73–74

Purpose How can you tell that water is a compound? This investigation will show that water is made from two different substances and is therefore a compound.

Setup	After 10 Minutes
wire connected to positive (+) terminal	
wire connected to negative (−) terminal	

Questions and Conclusions

1. Which of the wires had more bubbles around it? Identify the wire by telling whether it was connected to the positive (+) terminal or the negative (–) terminal.

_____

_____

2. Describe what you observed at the end of each wire after 10 minutes.

_____

_____

3. The gas you observe comes from the water. The electricity from the batteries breaks down the water into hydrogen gas and oxygen gas. How does this production of gases show that water is a compound?

_____

_____

Explore Further

Bend the two wires in the beaker upward. Fill two test tubes with salt water. Hold your thumb over the top of one test tube and turn it upside down. Put the test tube in the water and remove your thumb. Place the test tube over a wire. Repeat with the other test tube. What happens in each of the test tubes?

_____

_____

_____

3-2 Making Models of Atoms

Use with Investigation 3-2, pages 80–81

Purpose What three things must every atom have? You will make a model of an atom of a particular element in this investigation.

Name of Element:
Picture of Element:

Questions and Conclusions

1. What is the name of your element? _____

2. How many protons are in the nucleus? _____

3. How many neutrons does it have? _____

4. How many electrons does your element have? _____

5. Write at least four things that your model shows about atoms.

_____

_____

_____

Explore Further

Work with other students who have made models of different atoms. Find the mass number of each atom. The mass number is a number equal to the sum of the number of protons and neutrons in an atom. (You will learn more about mass number in the next lesson.) Put the atoms in order from lowest to highest mass number. What happens to the number of protons and neutrons as mass number increases?

_____

_____

_____

Exploring the Space Between Particles

Purpose   What is between particles? In this investigation, you will use volume to model space between atoms.

Materials   three 250-mL plastic beakers
marbles
sand
water
safety goggles

Procedure

1. Use the table below to record your data.

Stages of Experiment	Volume (mL)		
	Beaker A	Beaker B	Beaker C
at start of experiment			
after adding sand to beaker A			
after adding water to beaker A			

2. 🧤 Put on your safety goggles.

3. Label the beakers A, B, and C.

4. Fill beaker A with marbles to the 200-mL line. Do not let any marbles go above the 200-mL mark. Record in the data table the volume of the marbles.

5. Fill beaker B with sand to the 200-mL line. Record the volume.

6. Fill beaker C with water to the 200-mL line. Record the volume.

7. Pour some sand from beaker B into beaker A. Pour the sand to the 200-mL mark. Do not let any sand go above the 200-mL mark. Fill in the second row of the data table.

8. Pour water from beaker C into beaker A. Pour the water to the 200-mL mark. Do not let any water go above the 200-mL line. Fill in the third row of the data table.

Exploring the Space Between Particles, continued

Questions and Conclusions

1. What was the volume of marbles before you added sand or water to beaker A?

   _____

2. Did the marbles fill all of this space? How do you know?

   _____

   _____

   _____

3. What was the total volume of sand that you added to the beaker of marbles?
   (*Hint:* Subtract the volume of sand in beaker B after you added the sand to
   beaker A from the volume of sand before you added it.)

   _____

4. What was the total volume of water that you added to the beaker of marbles?
   (*Hint:* Subtract the volume of water in beaker C after you added the water
   to beaker A from the volume of water before you added it.)

   _____

5. What was the total volume of sand and water added to the marbles?
   (*Hint:* Add the volumes from questions 3 and 4.)

   _____

6. What is the volume of space that was present between the marbles before
   you added anything to beaker A? How do you know?

   _____

   _____

   _____

Explore Further

How did completing this activity help you understand the model of an atom?

_____

_____

_____

4-1 Finding Iron in Your Cereal

Use with Investigation 4-1, pages 95–96.

Purpose Do you think that iron-fortified cereal contains real bits of iron? In this investigation, you will observe bits of iron in an iron-fortified cereal.

Procedure Step	Observations
7	
8	
9	

Questions and Conclusions

1. What did you observe on the end of the magnet?

_____

2. What did you observe on the white paper?

_____

3. Were the bits on the white paper attracted to the magnet?

_____

4. What element from the cereal did you see?

_____

Explore Further

Why might iron be added to cereal? Use an encyclopedia or other reference source to find out.

_____

_____

_____

Exploring Elements

Purpose   Can elements be classified in different ways? In this investigation, you will identify data for different elements. You then will classify the elements based on their properties.

Materials   encyclopedia or other reference materials
index cards

Procedure

1. Use the data table to record information.

Element	Atomic Number	Atomic Mass	State (solid, liquid, or gas)	Color	Density (g/cm³)

2. Work in a group with four other students. Each student should choose five elements to research. Make sure no two group members choose the same element.

3. Research your five elements. Write in the data table the information you find about your elements.

4. Make an index card for each of your elements. Write the information from the data table on the card. Include any other information you think is important or interesting.

5. Gather all 25 cards from your group. See how many different ways you can classify the elements.

6. Choose one classification system that your group thinks is best.

Exploring Elements, continued

Questions and Conclusions

1. How many ways did you find to classify the elements?

_____

2. Did some ways work better than others? Why?

_____

_____

_____

3. Which classification system did your group think was best? Which properties did your group use to group the cards?

_____

_____

_____

_____

4. How could you make your classification system better?

_____

_____

_____

_____

Explore Further

Work with three other groups of five students to research the first 100 elements. Can you classify them the way you classified your 25 elements? Can you classify them the way any of the other groups classified their 25 elements? Are there any other ways you can classify elements?

_____

_____

_____

_____

Analyzing Common Compounds

Purpose   What elements are in common household products? In this investigation, you will examine the chemical makeup of common products in the home.

Materials   safety goggles   sugar
              hand lens   water
              salt   nail polish remover
              baking soda   vinegar

Procedure

1. Use the data table below to record your observations.

Compound	Chemical Name	Chemical Formula	Observations
salt	sodium chloride	NaCl	
baking soda	sodium bicarbonate	$NaHCO_3$	
sugar	sucrose	$C_6H_{12}O_2$	
water	hydrogen oxide	H_2O	
nail polish remover	acetone	CH_3COCH_3	
vinegar	acetic acid hydrate	$HC_2H_3O_2$	

2. [image] Put on your safety goggles.

3. Carefully observe a small amount of the salt. Record your observations in the table.

4. Repeat step 3 for the remaining materials. **Safety Alert: Do not breathe in the nail polish remover. Do not taste any of the materials.**

5. [image] [image] Return materials to proper waste collection site. Wash your hands as soon as your work area is clean.

Analyzing Common Compounds, continued

Questions and Conclusions

1. The chemical formula of a compound shows the symbols of the elements
   that are in the compound. What elements are in each of these compounds?
   Write them on the line.

   salt _____

   baking soda _____

   sugar _____

   water _____

   nail polish remover _____

   vinegar _____

2. Which compound has the most different elements?

3. Which compounds contain carbon?

   _____

4. Which element is present in all the compounds?

   _____

Explore Further

Sugar and nail polish remover are made of the same three elements—carbon,
hydrogen, and oxygen. Do these two substances have similar properties?
Why do you think sugar and nail polish remover are so different even though
they are made of the same elements?

_____

_____

_____

4-2 Electricity and Metals

Use with Investigation 4-2, pages 111–112

Purpose Do copper wire, sulfur, and aluminum all conduct electricity? In this investigation, you will identify materials that conduct electricity.

Materials	Observations
copper wires	
sulfur	
aluminum	
graphite (pencil lead)	

Questions and Conclusions

1. What happened to the lightbulb when you held the copper wires together?

_____

2. What happened to the lightbulb when you held the samples of sulfur and aluminum between the wires?

_____

3. What did you observe about the ability of copper, sulfur, and aluminum to conduct electricity?

_____

_____

4. Which materials do you think are metals? Explain your answer.

_____

_____

Explore Further

Pick up the pencil and hold it so the pencil lead is between the two unattached loops of wire. What happens? Can the pencil lead conduct electricity? Record your observations. Is the lead in the pencil a metal? Explain your answer.

_____

_____

5-1   Observing a Chemical Change

Use with Investigation 5-1, pages 121–122.

Purpose   Look at the descriptions of the three changes listed in the data table. Can you predict which will be a physical change and which will be a chemical change? In this investigation, you will observe physical and chemical changes.

Change	Appearance
washing soda in water	
Epsom salts in water	
washing soda and Epsom salts in water	

Questions and Conclusions

1. What happened when you added the washing soda to water?

_____

2. What happened when you added the Epsom salts to water?

_____

3. What did you observe when you mixed the contents of the jars together in step 6?

_____

_____

4. Did a chemical change or a physical change take place in steps 4 and 5? Explain your answer.

_____

_____

5. Did a chemical change or a physical change take place in step 6? Explain your answer.

_____

_____

Explore Further

Place a small amount of vinegar in a soft-drink bottle. Add a small amount of baking soda. Immediately cover the mouth of the bottle with a balloon. What do you observe happening? Did a chemical change take place? Explain your answer.

_____

Observing a Chemical Reaction

Purpose   Will the mixing of compounds result in a chemical reaction? In this investigation, you will observe a chemical reaction.

Materials   safety goggles
calcium chloride (CaCl)
baking soda (NaHCO$_3$)
spoon
locking plastic bag
small paper cup
water (H$_2$O)
graduated cylinder
paper towel

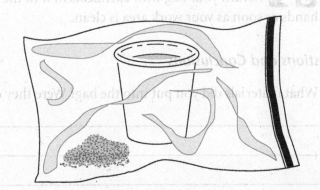

Procedure

1. Use the table below to record your data.

Steps	Description of Plastic Bag
before adding water	
after adding water	

2. Put on your safety goggles.

3. Place 2 spoonfuls of calcium chloride in the plastic bag.

4. Add 2 spoonfuls of baking soda to the calcium chloride in the plastic bag. Seal the bag. Shake it to mix the materials.

5. Use the graduated cylinder to measure 50 mL of water.

6. Pour the 50 mL of water into the paper cup. Wipe off the outside and the bottom of the cup with the paper towel. Open the plastic bag and carefully put the cup inside. Make sure that none of the powder gets wet. Seal the plastic bag.

7. Observe the contents of the bag. Record your observations in the first row of the data table.

Observing a Chemical Reaction, continued

8. Tip over the cup to spill the water into the bag. Make sure the powder gets wet. Write your observations in the second row of the data table.

9. [◇] [⚠] Return your bag with chemicals in it to the designated container. Wash your hands as soon as your work area is clean.

Questions and Conclusions

1. What materials did you put into the bag? Were they elements or compounds?

_____

_____

2. How did the contents of the bag change after you spilled the water?

_____

_____

3. Did a chemical reaction occur when you mixed the calcium chloride and the baking soda? How do you know?

_____

_____

_____

4. Did a chemical reaction occur when you mixed the water with the calcium chloride and the baking soda? How do you know?

_____

_____

Explore Further

Is it only the mixture of calcium chloride and baking soda together with water that results in a chemical reaction? Or will a chemical reaction result when water is added to each compound separately? Do an investigation to find out.

_____

_____

Exploring Acidity

Purpose How can you use litmus paper to tell whether substances are acids or bases? In this investigation, you identify substances as acids, bases, or neither acids nor bases.

Materials

safety goggles	6 small paper cups
salt	water
spoon	vinegar
drinking straw	milk
orange juice	antacid liquid
dish-washing liquid	blue litmus paper
red litmus paper	

Procedure

1. Use the table below to record your data.

Item	Effect on Red Litmus Paper	Effect on Blue Litmus Paper
salt water		
vinegar		
orange juice		
milk		
dish-washing liquid		
antacid liquid		

2. Put on your safety goggles.

3. Pour 1 spoonful of salt into a paper cup and fill the cup with water. Stir the mixture with the plastic straw to dissolve the salt.

4. Pour into separate paper cups a small amount of each of the remaining materials listed in the data table.

5. Take one of the sample cups. Dip a strip of red litmus paper and a strip of blue litmus paper into the sample. Hold the strips in the sample for 30 seconds. Then remove the strips. Write your observations in the data table.

6. Repeat step 5 for the remaining sample cups.

7. Return all chemicals to designated container. Wash your hands as soon as your work area is clean.

Exploring Acidity, continued

Questions and Conclusions

1. Did the orange juice affect the red litmus paper? If so, how?

_____

2. Did the orange juice affect the blue litmus paper? If so, how?

_____

3. Orange juice and vinegar are acids. How do acids affect red litmus paper?

_____

4. How do acids affect blue litmus paper?

_____

5. Dish-washing liquid and antacid liquid are bases. How do bases affect red litmus paper?

_____

6. How do bases affect blue litmus paper?

_____

7. Salt water and milk are not acids or bases. How do they affect red litmus paper?

_____

8. How do substances that are not acids or bases affect blue litmus paper?

_____

9. How can you use litmus paper to test for acids and bases?

_____

_____

_____

Explore Further

Make a chart identifying the substances you tested as acids, bases, or neither.
Test several other liquids and add them to your chart. Use another sheet of
paper for your chart.

5-2   Identifying Acids and Bases

Use with Investigation 5-2, pages 143–144.

Purpose   Read the substances listed in the data table. Can you identify which substances are acids and which are bases? In this investigation, you will use an indicator to test for acids and bases.

Substance	Color After Cabbage Juice Is Added	Acid or Base
baking soda		base
vinegar		acid
lemon juice		
weak ammonia		
aspirin		
soap		
soft drink		
milk of magnesia		

Questions and Conclusions

1. Which of the substances are acids?

_____

_____

2. Which of the substances are bases?

_____

_____

3. Are some bases stronger than others? Explain your answer.

_____

_____

_____

Explore Further

Use a piece of long-range litmus paper to test each substance. Record your results. How do your results compare with your previous results for each substance?

_____

_____

Speed of Dissolving

Purpose   What can affect how fast a solute dissolves? In this investigation, you will observe factors that may affect how quickly sugar dissolves.

Materials   safety goggles
4 beakers
water
4 sugar cubes
metal spoon
paper towel
clock with second hand

Procedure

1. Use the table to record your data.

| | Dissolving Time | |
	Crushed Sugar Cube	Whole Sugar Cube
stirred		
not stirred		

2. 🧤 Put on your safety goggles.

3. Fill each of the beakers with 100 mL of water.

4. Wrap one of the sugar cubes in a paper towel. Use the spoon to crush the sugar cubes into granules.

5. Pour the granules into one of the beakers of water. Stir with the spoon. Time how long it takes the granules to dissolve. Write the information in the data table.

6. Drop a whole sugar cube into another beaker of water. Stir. Time how long it takes the cube to dissolve. Write the information in the data table.

7. Repeat steps 4–6, but do not stir. (You may want to set a 5-minute time limit for each step.)

Speed of Dissolving, continued

Questions and Conclusions

1. In which beaker did the sugar dissolve faster—in the beaker with crushed sugar or in the beaker with the whole sugar cube?

_____

2. Look at the figures of the sugar cubes. One cube is whole. The other cube is broken into eight pieces. Use the figures to explain your answer to question 1.

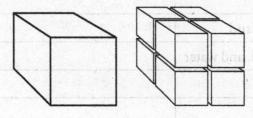

_____

_____

_____

_____

3. Did stirring affect the speed of dissolving? If so, how?

_____

_____

Explore Further

Many food products, such as instant tea and soup, come in powdered form. Why do you think this is so?

_____

_____

_____

6-1 Separating a Mixture

Use with Investigation 6-1, pages 153–154.

Purpose Look at the materials in the data table. Can you predict which material will be the solvent? Which material will be the solute? In this investigation, you will separate a mixture through dissolving.

Materials	Observations
salt	
sand	
mixture of salt and sand	
solution of salt, sand, and water	
filter paper	
sides of beaker	

Questions and Conclusions

1. In steps 5 and 6, what happened to the salt when you added water to the mixture?

_____

2. In step 6, did the sand dissolve? How do you know?

_____

3. In step 9, where was the salt after you poured the solution into the second beaker? How do you know?

_____

4. In step 9, which material remained on the filter paper?

_____

5. In step 11, what substance formed in the beaker?

_____

6. What is the solvent in this investigation? What is the solute?

_____

_____

Explore Further

Suppose you had a mixture of iron filings and sugar. How would you separate it? Write the procedure you would use on another sheet of paper.

Temperature and Chemical Reactions

Purpose   How does temperature affect the speed of a chemical reaction?
In this investigation, you will test and observe the effect of
temperature on a chemical reaction.

Materials   safety goggles
thermal gloves
2 balloons
2 one-hole rubber stoppers
2 flasks
250 mL hot water
250 mL cold water
4 antacid tablets
clock with second hand

Procedure

1. Use the table to record your data.

Time	Flask A (hot water)	Flask B (cold water)
beginning		
20 seconds		
40 seconds		
1 minute		
1 minute 20 seconds		
1 minute 40 seconds		
2 minutes		
2 minutes 20 seconds		
2 minutes 40 seconds		
3 minutes		

2. Read the entire procedure several times before beginning. Steps 8 and 9 will
happen very quickly. Be sure you know what to do.

3. Work with a partner. One of you should be the timer. The other will be the recorder.

4. Label the flasks *A* and *B*.

Temperature and Chemical Reactions, continued

5. Put on your safety goggles.

6. Stretch the mouth of each balloon around a rubber stopper. Make sure that the stoppers will still fit in the flasks after you attach the balloons.

7. Put on your thermal gloves. Fill flask A with 250 mL of hot water. Fill flask B with 250 mL of cold water. **Safety Alert: High Temperature**

8. Place one flask in front of you and the other flask in front of your partner. Hold a stopper in one hand and 2 antacid tablets in the other hand. Have your partner do the same. At exactly the same time, both of you should drop the tablets in the water and immediately put the stopper in the flask. Make sure the stoppers fit tightly.

9. As soon as the stoppers are in the flasks, the timer begins to time the experiment. Every 20 seconds, the timer says, "Now." When the timer says, "Now," the recorder writes down how full each balloon is. The timer may scribble notes quickly on a sheet of paper and later copy the notes onto the data table.

Questions and Conclusions

1. Did a chemical reaction occur in either of the flasks? How do you know?

_____

_____

2. Did water temperature affect what happened? If so, how?

_____

_____

3. How does heat affect the speed of a chemical reaction?

_____

_____

Explore Further

Suppose you added boiling water to a third flask. Would the chemical reaction be quicker than the reaction in Flask A? Explain your answer.

_____

_____

6-2 Observing Different Kinds of Reactions

Use with Investigation 6-2, pages 167–168.
Safety Alert: This activity should only be done as a Teacher Demonstration. Students should not do this activity on their own.

Purpose Can you predict the outcome of each reaction described on pages 167 and 168? In this investigation, you will study the four main types of chemical reactions.

Reaction	Observations
1	
2	
3	
4	

Questions and Conclusions

Complete the following table.

Reaction	Equation	Type of reaction
1	$4Fe + 3O_2 \rightarrow 2Fe_2O_3$	
2	$2H_2O_2 \rightarrow 2H_2O + O_2$	
3	$Fe + CuSO_4 \rightarrow FeSO_4 + Cu$	
4	$Na_2CO_3 + CaCl_2 \rightarrow 2NaCl + CaCO_3$	

Explore Further

Remember, the chemicals on the right side of the arrow are the products. In which of the above equations on the product (right) side, would you put an upward arrow? In which would you put a downward arrow?

_____

_____

7-1 Finding Speed

Use with Investigation 7-1, pages 185–186.

Purpose What formula would you use to calculate speed using distance and time? In this investigation, you will calculate speed by measuring distance and time and use a graph to show motion.

Length (meters)	Time (seconds)	Speed (distance/time)

Questions and Conclusions

1. Make a graph with distance in meters on the vertical (up-and-down) axis. Place time in seconds on the horizontal (left-to-right) axis. Extend the axes twice as far as you need to in order to graph your data. Plot one point where 0 seconds crosses 0 meters, to show the beginning of the roll. Plot a second point, using the distance and time values you recorded. Connect the two points with a straight line.

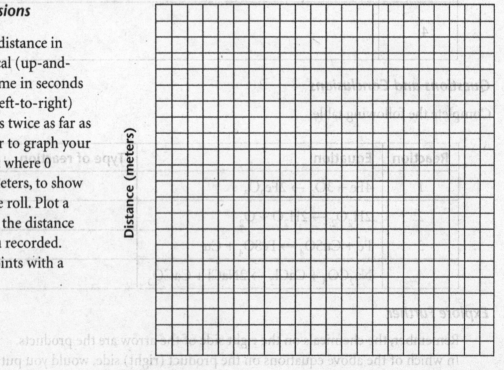

Distance (meters)

Time (seconds)

Finding Speed, continued

2. Use the graph you made to estimate the distance the marble traveled after it had been moving for half the recorded time.

_____

3. Extend the graph. Estimate the distance the marble would have gone if it had traveled for twice the recorded time.

_____

Explore Further

What do you think would happen if you stacked another book on top of the book that is under the ruler? How would the graph for this setup look? How would this graph be different from the graph you made?

_____

	How I Think the Cork Will Move	How the Cork Moved
started		
stopped		
turned right		
turned left		

Exploring Acceleration

Purpose   How does the motion of a bottle affect the motion of a cork inside the bottle? This investigation will examine changes in speed and direction.

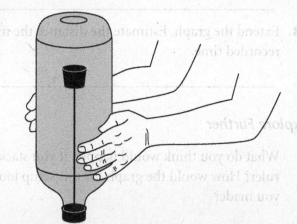

Materials   safety goggles
cork
needle
piece of thread, 20 cm long
2-L plastic soft-drink bottle with cap
masking tape
water

Procedure

1. Use the table to record your data.

Change in Motion	How I Think the Cork Will Move	How the Cork Moved
started		
stopped		
turned right		
turned left		

2. 🖐 Put on your safety goggles. **Safety Alert: Wear your safety glasses at all times. Use a folded cloth to hold the needle as you push it into the cork, or ask your teacher to push the needle into the cork.**

3. Insert the needle into the cork.

4. Thread the string through one end of the needle and tie it. Tape the other end of the thread to the inside of the bottle top, as shown in the figure above.

5. Fill the bottle with water.

Exploring Acceleration, continued

6. Lower the cork into the bottle. Place the top on the bottle. Make sure all the thread is inside the bottle. Screw the bottle cap on tightly.

7. Look at the motions described in the first column of the data table. How do you think the cork will move if you carry the bottle upside down and perform each of the movements? Write your predictions in the second column of the data table.

8. Carefully turn the bottle upside down.

9. Hold the bottle at arm's length so you can easily see the cork. Move around the room, changing your speed and direction quickly. For example, start walking quickly. Next, stop walking quickly. Walk forward, then suddenly step to the left. Each time you change your motion, observe the cork. Write your observations in the data table.

Questions and Conclusions

1. When you suddenly moved forward, what did the cork do?

   _____

   _____

2. When you moved forward and then stopped, what did the cork do?

   _____

   _____

3. When you turned right, what did the cork do?

   _____

   _____

4. When you turned left, what did the cork do?

   _____

   _____

Explore Further

How would you explain the reasons for the ways the cork moved?

   _____

   _____

Newton's First Law of Motion

Purpose   How do forces affect objects at rest and objects in motion? In this investigation, you will observe the first law of motion.

Materials   safety goggles
shoe box
scissors
tennis ball
index card
quarter

Procedure

1. Use the table to record your data.

Objects	Observations
tennis ball	
quarter	

2. 👓 Put on your safety goggles. **Safety Alert: Wear your safety goggles at all times.**

3. ✂ Cut one end from the side of the shoe box, as shown in the figure below. **Safety Alert: Carry the scissors with the blades pointed down. Use the scissors carefully as you cut the box.**

4. Place the shoe box on the floor with the open end pointing toward a wall. Place the tennis ball inside the box opposite the opening you made.

5. Rapidly push the box toward the wall. Then stop the box suddenly. Observe what happens to the ball. Write your observations in the data table.

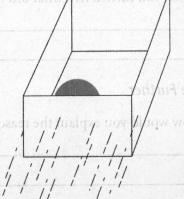

Newton's First Law of Motion, continued

6. Place the index card on the edge of a table. Make sure some of it extends over the edge of the table.

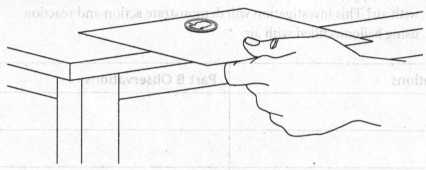

7. Place the quarter on the index card.

8. Quickly pull the index card straight out from the table. Observe what happens to the quarter. Write your observations in the data table.

Questions and Conclusions

1. In step 5, when you started moving the box, what happened to the ball?

_____

2. In step 5, when you stopped pushing the box, what happened to the ball?

_____

3. When you placed the quarter on the index card, neither the card nor the quarter was moving. What happened when you moved the index card?

_____

_____

Explore Further

Explain how this activity demonstrates Newton's first law of motion.

_____

_____

_____

_____

7-2 Newton's Third Law of Motion

Use with Investigation 7-2, pages 199–200.

Purpose What happens when you release a balloon that is filled with air? This investigation will demonstrate action and reaction using balloons filled with air.

Part A Observations	Part B Observations

Questions and Conclusions

1. In Part A, in what direction does the escaping air move?

_____

2. In Part A, in what direction does the balloon move?

_____

3. How does Part A demonstrate Newton's third law of motion?

_____

_____

4. In Part B, in what direction do the balloons move?

_____

5. In Part B, describe the directions of the forces to explain what the balloons do.

_____

_____

Explore Further

In Part A, if you attached a weight to the balloon, how would that affect its motion?

_____

_____

8-1 Mass, Height, and Energy

Use with Investigation 8-1, pages 216–217.

Purpose Does an object's mass have an effect on its potential and kinetic energy? This investigation will demonstrate how mass affects potential and kinetic energy.

Object	Distance Cup Moved
small marble	
large marble	
small marble	
large marble	

Questions and Conclusions

1. Which marble pushed the cup farther from the ramp?

_____

_____

2. What conclusion can you draw about the effect of mass on kinetic energy?

_____

_____

_____

Explore Further

How does the height of the ramp affect potential energy? Repeat the investigation using ramps of different heights. Record the results in the data table.

_____

8-2 Finding the Mechanical Advantage of a Lever

Use with Investigation 8-2, pages 227–228.

Purpose Which fulcrum position would have a greater mechanical advantage—one at 20 cm or one at 80 cm? In this investigation, you will find the mechanical advantage of a lever.

Fulcrum Position	Resistance Force	Effort Force	Resistance Arm	Effort Arm
50 cm				
80 cm				
20 cm				

Questions and Conclusions

1. Where was the fulcrum placed when you had to apply the most force? Where was it placed when you had to apply the least force?

   _____

   _____

2. Calculate the mechanical advantage of the three levers using the formula $MA = \dfrac{\text{effort arm}}{\text{resistance arm}}$.

   _____

3. Which setup showed the greatest mechanical advantage? Which setup showed the least?

   _____

   _____

4. How do the mechanical advantages you calculated in step 3 compare to your answers to question 1?

   _____

   _____

5. Explain how the position of the fulcrum affects a lever's mechanical advantage.

   _____

   _____

Finding the Mechanical Advantage of a Lever, continued

Explore Further

Repeat the investigation steps, but use a weight with a different mass. Record your observations. Explain how a weight's mass affects mechanical advantage.

Exploring Pulleys

Purpose   How would the number of pulleys used to lift a mass affect the force and the distance required? In this investigation, you will investigate how pulleys affect work.

Materials   safety goggles
masking tape
2 metersticks
2 chairs
3 pulleys
string
50-g mass
10-g mass
spring scale

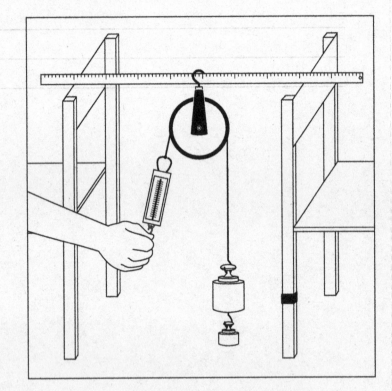

Procedure

1. Use the table to record your data.

	Force	Distance
1 pulley		
2 pulleys		
3 pulleys		

2. Put on your safety goggles. Place a piece of masking tape on the leg of one of the chairs. The tape should be 20 cm above the floor.

3. Place one meterstick across two chairs as shown in the figure above. Hook a pulley onto the meterstick.

4. Hook the 10-g mass to the 50-g mass. Attach one end of the string to the 50-g mass.

5. Feed the string through the pulley. Attach the other end of the string to the spring scale.

Exploring Pulleys, continued

6. Pull the spring scale slowly and smoothly. Pull until the masses are 20 cm above the floor. Use the piece of masking tape you placed on the chair leg as a guide to let you know when the masses are at the proper height. Notice the reading on the spring scale. This reading tells the force that is needed to pull the masses. Record the force in the first column of the data table.

7. Measure the length of string between the spring scale and the pulley. Write the information in the second column of the data table.

8. Repeat steps 5–7, using two pulleys.

9. Repeat steps 5–7 again, using three pulleys.

Questions and Conclusions

1. How much force was required to lift the masses, using one pulley?

_____

2. How much force was required to lift the weights, using two pulleys?

_____

3. What rule can you make up that involves mass, force, and the number of pulleys?

_____

_____

4. How far did you pull the scale, using one pulley?

_____

5. How far did you pull the scale, using three pulleys?

_____

6. What rule can you make up that involves distance, force, and the number of pulleys?

_____

_____

Explore Further

How does a movable pulley differ from a fixed pulley? Which changes the direction of the effort force? Which changes the effort force? Set up both kinds of systems and use each to lift a mass.

_____

_____

Exploring an Inclined Plane

Purpose   How would using an inclined plane to lift a mass affect the force and the distance factors? In this investigation, you will investigate how an inclined plane affects work.

Materials   safety goggles
skateboard
spring scale
string
board, 2-m long
meterstick

Procedure

1. Use the table to record your data.

	Force	Distance
without inclined plane		
with inclined plane		

2. 👓 Put on your safety goggles. Work with a partner. Use the string to attach the skateboard to the spring scale.

3. Lean the board against the desk. It should be at about a 45-degree angle. The slanted board is an inclined plane. Place the skateboard on the bottom of the board. One partner should slowly raise the spring scale up the board until the skateboard is even with the top of the desk. The other partner should read the scale. The reading on the spring scale tells the force used. Write the force in the first column of the data table.

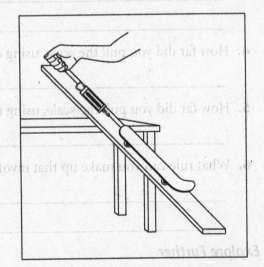

Exploring an Inclined Plane, continued

4. Place the skateboard on the floor next to your desk. One partner should slowly raise the spring scale until the skateboard is even with the top of the desk. The other partner should read the scale. Write the reading in the first column of the data table.

5. Measure the distance from the floor to the desktop. Then measure the length of the board from the floor to the desktop. Use this information to complete the data table.

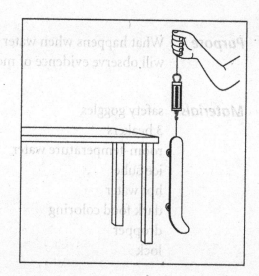

Questions and Conclusions

1. How did using an inclined plane affect the amount of force needed to raise the skateboard?

2. How did the inclined plane affect the distance the skateboard traveled?

_____

_____

_____

Explore Further

Try leaning the board against other surfaces at differing angles less than 45 degrees. (You could use books stacked to different heights to make a surface. Use a protractor to measure the angle of the board.) Measure the force required to lift the skateboard up the board. How does the angle of a ramp affect force required?

_____

_____

_____

Exploring Heat and Motion of Particles

Purpose   What happens when water particles move? In this investigation, you will observe evidence of motion in water and investigate how heat affects it.

Materials   safety goggles
3 beakers
room-temperature water
ice cube
hot water
dark food coloring
dropper
lock

Procedure

1. Use the table below to record your data.

Beaker	Observations
A	
B	
C	

2. 🥽 Put on your safety goggles. Label the beakers A, B, and C.

3. Pour 250 mL of room-temperature water into beaker A. Place the ice cube in the water. Wait 3 minutes.

4. Pour 250 mL of room-temperature water into beaker B.

5. 🧤 Put on your thermal gloves. Pour 250 mL of hot water into beaker C. **Safety Alert: High Temperature.**

Exploring Heat and the Motion of Particles, continued

6. Take the ice cube out of beaker A.

7. As soon as the water has stopped moving in all three beakers, place 1 drop of food coloring in the middle of each beaker. Wait 3 minutes.

8. Observe all 3 beakers. Write your observations in the data table.

Questions and Conclusions

1. What did you observe happening in each of the beakers?

   _____

   _____

2. Based on what you observed in this activity, do you think the particles of water are still or moving? Explain your answer.

   _____

   _____

   _____

3. How does heat affect the motion of the particles?

   _____

   _____

   _____

Explore Further

Watch this teacher demonstration. The teacher places a beaker of cold water on a burner. After the water is still, the teacher adds a drop of food coloring into the beaker and slowly heats the beaker. What do you observe? Explain why you observed this.

   _____

   _____

   _____

9-1 Observing and Comparing Expansion and Contraction

Use with Investigation 9-1, pages 247–248.

Purpose What happens when a gas expands and contracts? In this investigation, you will observe and compare expansion and contraction of gases.

Environment	Changes in Balloon
in warm water	
in cold water	
at room temperature	

Questions and Conclusions

1. What happened to the balloon when the flask was heated?

_____

_____

2. What happened to the balloon as the flask cooled?

_____

_____

3. What caused the changes you observed in the balloon?

_____

_____

Explore Further

Explain what would happen to a helium-filled balloon if it was moved to a colder room. Explain what would happen to the balloon if it was moved to a warmer room.

_____

_____

9-2   Measuring the Rate of Heat Loss

Use with Investigation 9-2, pages 260–261.

Purpose   Do different amounts of water cool at different rates? In this investigation, you will measure the cooling rates of different amounts of water.

Time	Temperature (°C)	
	Large Jar	**Small Jar**
0 minutes		
1 minute		
2 minutes		
3 minutes		
4 minutes		
5 minutes		
6 minutes		
7 minutes		
8 minutes		
9 minutes		
10 minutes		
11 minutes		
12 minutes		
13 minutes		
14 minutes		
15 minutes		

Questions and Conclusions

1. What was the temperature of the water in each jar the first time you measured it? After 8 minutes? After 15 minutes?

_____

_____

2. How did the amount of water in the jar affect how fast the temperature of the water dropped?

_____

_____

Measuring the Rate of Heat Loss, continued

3. What happened to the heat from the water as the water cooled?

_____

_____

Explore Further

Repeat the activity, using a jar of ice water. Then answer these questions.

1. How did the temperature of the water change after 8 minutes? After 15 minutes?

_____

_____

2. Explain the change of temperature that occurred in the ice water.

_____

_____

_____

Exploring Heat Absorption

Purpose   How does color affect absorption of heat? In this lesson, you will investigate the effects of color on heat absorption.

Materials   safety goggles
2 empty frozen juice cans
black construction paper
white construction paper
scissors
tape

water
black cardboard
white cardboard
2 thermometers
sunlight or 2 lamps with 100-watt bulbs

Procedure

1. Use the table below to record your data.

Time	Black Can	White Can
beginning		
3 minutes		
6 minutes		
9 minutes		
12 minutes		
15 minutes		
18 minutes		
21 minutes		

2. 🖐 Put on your safety goggles. **Safety Alert: Avoid contact with the light sources, which may be hot.** Cover one of the cans with black paper, as shown in the figure on the next page. Cover the other can with white paper.

3. Fill both of the cans with water.

4. Cut a square of black paper large enough to cover the top of the black can. Carefully poke a hole in the middle of the square. Insert a thermometer through the hole. Place the square over the top of the black can. The bottom of the thermometer should be in the center of the can.

Exploring Heat Absorption, continued

5. Repeat step 4, using the white cardboard and the white can.

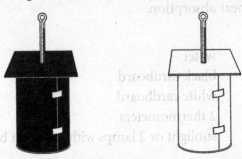

6. Place the cans in strong sunlight. If that is not possible, place a lamp with a 100-watt lightbulb next to each can. The light should be shining directly on the cans. The bulbs should be as close to the cans as possible.

7. Read the temperature of the water in each can. Write the information in the data table.

8. Repeat step 7 every 3 minutes, and record your observations in the table.

Questions and Conclusions

1. What is the source of energy that heats the cans?

_____

2. Which can absorbed more heat?

_____

3. How does color affect how an object absorbs heat?

_____

_____

4. Why would a person stay cooler in summer by wearing light-colored clothing?

_____

_____

_____

Explore Further

Based on your observations, what color clothing would keep people cool in the summer? Explain your answer.

_____

_____

Making Musical Sounds

Purpose   What causes sounds to be higher or lower in pitch? In this investigation, you will produce the notes of the musical scale.

Materials   8 empty 16-oz glass bottles
masking tape
water
graduated cylinder

Procedure

1. Use the table below to record your data.

Bottle	Amount of Water (mL)	What the Sound Is Like
1	none	
2	93	
3	151	
4	215	
5	277	
6	315	
7	348	
8	374	

2. Label each bottle with a number from 1 to 8.

3. Put no water in bottle 1. In bottle 2, put 93 mL of water.

4. Blow across the opening of the bottle to produce a musical sound. Write a description of this sound in the data table.

5. Add 151 mL of water to bottle 3. Blow across the opening to produce a musical sound. How does this sound compare with the sound produced by bottle 2? Record your observations in the data table.

6. Fill the remaining bottles with the amount of water shown in the table.

7. Blow across the opening of each bottle to produce a tone of the musical scale. Each bottle will produce a different note of the scale. You may need to practice to obtain good results.

Making Musical Sounds, continued

8. You can change the pitch of the notes by adding or removing water from the bottle. Adjust the amount of water in each bottle until the sounds you make with the bottles resemble a musical scale.

9. Try playing the following familiar tunes by blowing across the numbered bottle. The R indicates a rest between notes.

Tune A													
1	1	5	5	6	6	5	R	4	4	3	3	2	2	1

Tune B

8 8 5 5 3 3 1   1 5 4 3 2 1

Questions and Conclusions

1. What is the name of each tune?

    Tune A: _____

    Tune B: _____

2. What must you do to make the pitch of the bottle higher?

    _____

    _____

3. What must you do to make the pitch of the bottle lower?

    _____

    _____

Explore Further

Observe musicians playing instruments, such as flutes and tubas. Listen to the pitch of the sounds each instrument makes. Study the size and shape of the instrument. What do you think causes the difference in pitch?

_____

_____

10-1 Inferring How Sound Waves Travel

Use with Investigation 10-1, pages 287–288.

Purpose Can sound waves travel through matter? This investigation will demonstrate that sound waves are vibrations that travel through matter.

How the Rubber Band Was Plucked	Observations

Questions and Conclusions

1. In Step 7, what happened to the salt when you plucked the rubber band?
_____
_____

2. What do you think caused the salt to move? Explain your answer.
_____
_____
_____

3. In Step 8, how did the force you used to pluck the rubber band affect the sound it made?
_____
_____

4. In Step 8, how did the force you used to pluck the rubber band affect the salt on the plastic wrap?
_____
_____

Explore Further

1. Use a tuning fork and a plastic beaker half-filled with water. Gently tap the tuning fork against the heel of your hand and place the tips of the fork into the beaker of water. What happens to the water?
_____

2. Vary the force used to tap the tuning fork. Notice what happens to the water as you vary the force.
_____

Making a Pinhole Camera

Purpose How does an image look on the lens of a pinhole camera? In this investigation, you will make a pinhole camera to investigate the sharpness and position of images seen in the camera.

Materials safety glasses
empty oatmeal box
waxed paper
rubber band
pin

Procedure

1. Use the table to record your data.

Observations		
Object pointed at	With small hole	With large hole

2. Put on your safety glasses. Take the lid off the oatmeal box. Spread the waxed paper over the opening of the box. The waxed paper should be tight and smooth. Hold the waxed paper in place with the rubber band, as shown in the figure above.

3. Use the pin to poke a hole in the bottom of the oatmeal box. The hole should be in the center of the bottom of the box. **Safety Alert: Handle the pin carefully to avoid injury.**

4. To use your pinhole camera, point the bottom of the box at a brightly lit object. Look at the waxed paper. How good is the image you see? Record your observations in the data table. What is the position of the image? Record your observations.

Making a Pinhole Camera, continued

5. Repeat step 4 with at least 4 more bright objects.

6. Make the hole in your pinhole camera a little bigger. How does that change the image? Keep making the hole a little bigger and checking the image. Record your observations in the data table.

Questions and Conclusions

1. How are the real objects different from their images in the camera?

   _____

   _____

2. How could you increase the quality of the images?

   _____

   _____

3. What happens to the image as the hole gets bigger?

   _____

   _____

Explore Further

What happens if you use different sizes and kinds of containers or different materials in place of the waxed paper? Make another camera from some of these materials and find out.

   _____

   _____

   _____

   _____

Physical Science

10-2 # Measuring Angles of Reflected Rays

Use with Investigation 10-2, pages 299–300

Purpose Does the angle of a light ray when it hits a mirror match the angle of its reflection? In this investigation, you will measure the angles at which a light ray hits and is reflected from a mirror.

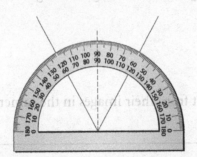

Trial	Angle A	Angle B
1		
2		
3		

Questions and Conclusions

1. Which angle—A or B—shows the angle at which the light traveled to the mirror?

_____

2. Which angle shows the angle at which the light was reflected from the mirror?

_____

3. How do angles A and B compare?

_____

_____

Explore Further

On a piece of paper write the word AMBULANCE backwards as shown below.
Hold the paper up to a mirror. How are the letters reflected in the mirror?

ƎƆИA⅃UᗺMA

_____

_____

_____

Exploring Electric Charges

Purpose What happens when you rub two different kinds of materials together? In this investigation, you will observe how an electric charge affects the way an object behaves.

Materials safety goggles
meterstick
masking tape
2 balloons
string
wool cloth

Procedure

1. Use the table to record your data.

Steps	Objects	What I Think Will Happen	What Happened
5–6			
7–8			
9			
10–11			

2. 🖐 Put on your safety goggles. Tape the meterstick to the top of your desk. Make sure it extends over the edge.

3. Blow up one of the balloons. Tie the end of the balloon shut. Attach one end of the string to the balloon. Use the other end of the string to hang the balloon from the meterstick.

4. Hold the piece of wool cloth away from the balloon.

5. What do you think will happen if you move the wool toward the balloon? Record your prediction in the data table.

6. Slowly move the wool cloth close to the balloon. Observe what happens. Write your observations in the data table.

7. Rub the balloon with the wool cloth for 30 seconds. Move the wool cloth away from the balloon. What do you think will happen if you move the cloth toward the balloon? Record your prediction in the data table.

Exploring Electric Charges, continued

8. Slowly move the wool cloth toward the balloon. Observe what happens. Write your observations in the data table.

9. Blow up the second balloon. Move it toward the first balloon. Observe what happens. Record you observations.

10. Rub the second balloon with the wool cloth. What do you think will happen if you move this balloon toward the first balloon? Record you prediction.

11. Hold the second balloon away from the first balloon. Move the second balloon slowly toward the first balloon. Observe what happens. Record your observations.

Questions and Conclusions

1. Did the wool cloth or the balloons have a charge before they were rubbed together? How do you know?

_____

_____

2. Did the balloons and the cloth have a charge after they were rubbed together? How do you know?

_____

_____

3. How did the balloon and the wool cloth affect each other after they were rubbed together? What does this tell about the charge on each object?

_____

_____

4. How did the two balloons affect each other after they were rubbed? What does this tell you about the charge on the balloons?

_____

_____

Explore Further

Explain what happened to electrons when you performed steps 8 and 11.

_____

_____

Identifying Electric Conductors

Purpose   What solutions are good conductors of electricity? In this investigation, you will explore how various solutions conduct electricity.

Materials

safety goggles	8 paper cups
graduated cylinder	baking soda
spoon	4 drinking straws
salt	sugar
mineral oil	orange juice
rubbing alcohol	vinegar
dry-cell battery	lightbulb and holder
3 wires with insulation removed from the ends	2 nails water

Procedure

1. Use the table to record your data.

Material	Prediction	Observations	Conductor or Nonconductor
baking soda			
salt			
sugar			
mineral oil			
orange juice			
rubbing alcohol			
vinegar			
water			
other			

2. For each of the materials in the table, predict whether it is a conductor or a nonconductor. Write your prediction in the data table.

3. Put on your safety goggles. Pour 125 mL of water into each of 4 cups.

4. Pour $\frac{1}{2}$ spoonful of baking soda into one of the cups of water. Stir with a drinking straw until the baking soda dissolves.

Identifying Electric Conductors, continued

5. Repeat step 4 with the salt.

6. Repeat step 4 with the sugar.

7. Pour the orange juice, mineral oil, rubbing alcohol, and vinegar into the remaining cups. One liquid should go in each cup.

8. Attach one end of a wire to one battery terminal and the other end to the bulb holder. Attach one end of the second wire to the bulb holder. Wrap the loose end of the second wire around a nail. Attach one end of the third wire to the other battery terminal. Wrap the loose end of the third wire around the other nail.

9. Dip the two nails into the liquid in the cup with the baking soda. Make sure the nails do not touch each other. Observe what happens to the lightbulb. Record your observations in the data table.

10. Repeat step 9, using each of the remaining cups.

11. [icons] Return all solutions to the designated waste container. Wash your hands as soon as your work area is clean.

Questions and Conclusions

1. If the lightbulb glows brightly, the material is a good conductor. If the lightbulb glows faintly, the material is a poor conductor. If the lightbulb does not glow at all, the material is a nonconductor. Complete the data table by telling whether each material is a good conductor or a nonconductor.

2. How do your predictions about which materials are conductors compare to the actual results?

   _____

   _____

3. Which material made the light shine the brightest?

   _____

Explore Further

Do you think distilled, or purified, water would conduct electricity differently from the way tap water does? Explain your answer.

_____

_____

11-1 Constructing Series Circuits

Use with Investigation 11-1, pages 333–334.

Purpose How would you create a series circuit? In this investigation, you will construct and study a series circuit.

Circuit	Schematic Diagram	Prediction	Observations
A			
B			
C			

Questions and Conclusions

1. What items make up circuit A? What kind of circuit is it?

_____

_____

2. What items make up circuit B? What kind of circuit is it?

_____

_____

_____

Constructing Series Circuits, continued

3. How brightly did the bulbs in circuit B shine compared to the bulb in circuit A? Explain your answer.

_____

_____

_____

4. What happened in circuit B when one of the bulbs was unscrewed? Why did that happen?

_____

_____

_____

5. How brightly did the bulbs in circuit C shine compared to the bulbs in circuit B? Explain your answer.

_____

_____

_____

Explore Further

What do you think would happen if you added more bulbs or batteries to your circuit? Write your prediction on a sheet of paper. Then construct a circuit and find out. Record your observations.

_____

_____

11-2   Constructing Parallel Circuits

Use with Investigation 11-2, pages 338–339

Purpose   How do you know a circuit is a parallel circuit? In the investigation, you will construct and study parallel circuits.

Circuit	Schematic Diagram	Prediction	Observations
A			
B			
C			
D			
E			

Constructing Parallel Circuits, continued

Questions and Conclusions

1. What items make up circuit C? What kind of circuit is it?

   _____

2. Are the cells in circuit E connected in series or in parallel?

3. How brightly did the bulbs in circuit B shine compared to the bulbs in circuit A? Why?

   _____

4. What happened in circuit C when various bulbs were unscrewed?

   _____

   _____

5. How brightly did the bulbs in circuit D shine compared to the bulbs in circuit A? Why?

   _____

   _____

6. How brightly did the bulbs in circuit E shine compared to the bulbs in circuit D? Why?

   _____

   _____

Explore Further

Which circuit—A or B—will stay lit longer? Which uses less energy for a given amount of time?

_____

_____

Exploring Magnetism

Purpose   What materials can block a magnetic field? In this investigation, you will identify which materials, if any, can block a magnetic field.

Materials   safety goggles   support stand
                 clamp   rod
                 bar magnet   thread
                 paper clip   metric ruler
                 sheet of paper   copper sheet
                 cotton fabric   aluminum foil
                 plastic wrap   plywood

Procedure

1. Use the table to record your data.

Material	Does it block a magnetic field?
sheet of paper	
copper sheet	
cotton fabric	
aluminum foil	
plastic wrap	
plywood	

2. 🧤 Put on your safety goggles. Clamp the rod onto the support stand.

3. Place the bar magnet on the desktop some distance from the support stand, as shown in the figure.

4. Tie one end of the thread around the paper clip. Tie the other end to the rod. Make sure that the paper clip is attracted to the bar magnet. Tighten the thread to leave a 3-cm gap between the paper clip and the magnet.

Exploring Magnetism, continued

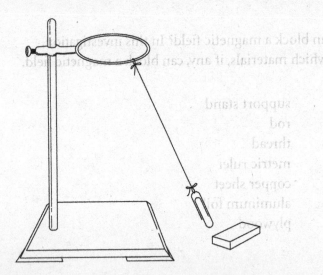

5. Place the sheet of paper between the magnet and the paper clip. If the material blocks the magnetic field, the paper clip will hang straight down. Record your observations in the data table.

6. Repeat step 5, using each of the remaining materials.

7. Repeat step 5 again, using two other materials you choose.

Questions and Conclusions

1. Which materials blocked the magnetic field?

_____

_____

2. What rule can you make up about blocking a magnetic field?

_____

_____

Explore Further

A magnetic window cleaner makes it possible for a person to clean the inside and the outside of a window at the same time. Describe how it might work. (Hint: Glass does not block magnets.)

_____

_____

_____

12-1 Observing Magnetic Lines of Force

Use with Investigation 12-1, pages 354–355.

Purpose Do the lines of force around a bar magnet look different
than the lines of force around a horseshoe magnet?
In this investigation, you will observe the lines of force
around two magnets.

Part	Bar Magnet	Horseshoe Magnet
A		
B		
C		

Questions and Conclusions

1. Describe the pattern made by the lines of force of the single bar magnet.

_____

_____

2. In Part B, did the poles of the bar magnets attract or repel each other?
How did the lines of force show this?

_____

_____

3. In Part C, did the poles of the bar magnets attract or repel each other? How do you know?

_____

_____

_____

Observing Magnetic Lines of Force, continued

4. How were the patterns on the bar magnet similar to those on the horseshoe magnet?

_____

_____

Explore Further

Find a metal bar that is attracted to a magnet. Repeat Parts B and C using the metal bar. Record your observations.

_____

_____

_____

_____

Experimenting with a Compass

Purpose   How can you make a simple compass? What materials will affect it? In this investigation, you will make a compass and observe what materials affect it.

Materials   safety goggles   bar magnet
small piece of sponge   correction fluid
tray   water
magnetic compass   crumpled paper ball
iron nail   wooden pencil
steel paper clip   eraser
needle

Procedure

1. Use the table below to record your data.

Material	Does it affect the compass?
paper ball	
iron nail	
wooden pencil	
paper clip	
eraser	

2. 🫁 Put on your safety goggles. Rub one end of the bar magnet along the needle. Rub it in the same direction 25 times. **Safety Alert: Handle the needle carefully to avoid poking yourself.**

3. Find an object in the classroom that is attracted to the magnet. Use this object to test the needle. The object should be attracted to the needle, too. If the needle does not attract the object, repeat step 2.

4. Slide the needle through the sponge so that it sticks out on each end. Use the correction fluid to paint one end of the needle white.

5. Fill the tray with water. Float the sponge in the water. Keep the bar magnet away from the needle. If it floats freely, one end of the needle should point toward Earth's magnetic north pole. Use a compass to check your magnet.

Experimenting with a Compass, continued

6. Gently spin the sponge. Observe what happens.

7. Move the crumpled paper around near the needle. Record your observations in the data table.

8. Repeat step 5, using each of the other materials.

9. Repeat step 5 again, using two materials you choose.

Questions and Conclusions

1. In step 6, what happened to the needle after you spun the sponge? Why do you think this happened?

_____

_____

_____

_____

2. Which materials affected the compass?

_____

_____

3. Which materials did not affect the compass?

_____

_____

_____

Explore Further

Use your compass to give directions to a particular place.

_____

_____

_____

12-2 Constructing an Electromagnet

Use with Investigation 12-2, pages 367–368.

Purpose Is it possible to increase an electromagnet's magnetic properties? In this investigation, you will see how to increase the magnetic properties of an electromagnet.

Number of Turns of Wire Coil	Number of Paper Clips
5	
10	
15	
25	

Questions and Conclusions

1. In step 7, what happened to the paper clips when you removed one end of the wire from the battery?

_____

_____

_____

2. How did the number of coils in the wire affect the electromagnet?

_____

_____

_____

Constructing an Electromagnet, continued

Explore Further

1. Sprinkle iron filings on a sheet of paper. Hold the paper over the wire when the coil has 25 turns of the wire. Describe the pattern made by the iron filings.

_____

_____

2. Hold the paper with the iron filings over the wire coil when it has 10 turns of the wire. How does the pattern made by the iron filings compare with the pattern you saw in step 1?

_____

_____

3. How does the number of turns in the wire coil affect the magnetic force around the wire?

_____

_____

4. What would happen if you used two batteries in series?

_____

_____

_____

_____

_____

SAFETY SYMBOLS

These symbols warn of possible dangers in the laboratory and remind you to work carefully.

 Safety Goggles Wear safety goggles to protect your eyes in any activity involving chemicals, flames or heating, or glassware.

 Lab Apron Wear a laboratory apron to protect your skin and clothing from damage.

 Breakage Handle breakable materials, such as glassware, with care. Do not touch broken glassware.

 Heat-Resistant Gloves Use an oven mitt or other hand protection when handling hot materials, such as hot plates or hot glassware.

 Plastic Gloves Wear disposable plastic gloves when working with harmful chemicals and organisms. Keep your hands away from your face, and dispose of the gloves according to your teacher's instructions.

 Heating Use a clamp or tongs to pick up hot glassware. Do not touch hot objects with your bare hands.

 Flames Before you work with flames, tie back loose hair and clothing. Follow instructions from your teacher about lighting and extinguishing flames.

 No Flames When using flammable materials, make sure there are no flames, sparks, or other exposed heat sources present.

 Corrosive Chemical Avoid getting acid or other corrosive chemicals on your skin or clothing or in your eyes. Do not inhale the vapors. Wash your hands after the activity.

 Poison Do not let any poisonous chemical come into contact with your skin, and do not inhale its vapors. Wash your hands when you are finished with the activity.

SAFETY SYMBOLS (continued)

 Fumes Work in a well-ventilated area when harmful vapors may be involved. Avoid inhaling vapors directly. Only test an odor when directed to do so by your teacher, and use a wafting motion to direct the vapor toward your nose.

 Sharp Object Scissors, scalpels, knives, needles, pins, and tacks can cut your skin. Always direct a sharp edge or point away from yourself and others.

 Electric Shock To avoid electric shock, never use electrical equipment around water, or when the equipment is wet or your hands are wet. Be sure cords are untangled and cannot trip anyone. Unplug equipment not in use.

 Physical Safety When an experiment involves physical activity, avoid injuring yourself or others. Alert your teacher if there is any reason you should not participate.

 Disposal Dispose of chemicals and other laboratory materials safely. Follow the instructions from your teacher.

 Hand Washing Wash your hands thoroughly when finished with an activity. Use soap and warm water. Rinse well.

 General Safety Awareness When this symbol appears, follow the instructions provided. When you are asked to develop your own procedure in a lab, have your teacher approve your plan before you go further.